PCI DSS
A Pocket Guide

PCI DSS
A Pocket Guide

Second edition

ALAN CALDER
NICKI CARTER

IT Governance Publishing

FOREWORD

Target dates for compliance with the PCI DSS itself have all long since passed. Many organisations – particularly those that fall below the top tier of payment card transaction volumes – – are not yet compliant.

There are perhaps three reasons for this.

The first is that PCI DSS has no legal status: it is not a law and does not have the force of law. Enforcement can only be carried out by contractual means, in a competitive payment card market place.

The second is that enforcement is driven by the card payment brands, through the banks that have the commercial relationships with the merchants that are supposed to comply. Enforcement is inconsistent at best and non-existent at worst.

The third is that PCI DSS is extremely prescriptive, and takes a determined one-size-fits-all approach to information security requirements. Compliance is therefore seen as both expensive and bureaucratic.

It is not surprising, therefore, that merchants try and avoid compliance with this standard. This is a short-sighted and high risk stance to adopt – rather like assuming that your business has no exposure to acts of nature or IT failure and doesn't, therefore, require a business or IT service continuity plan.

All businesses that accept payment cards are prey for hackers and criminal gangs that seek to steal payment card and individual identity details. Many attacks are highly automated, seeking out website and payment card system vulnerabilities remotely, using increasingly sophisticated tools and techniques. When a vulnerability is discovered, an attack can start – without management or staff of the target company having any awareness of what is going on.

When the attack is exposed – perhaps through a victim disputing fraudulent credit card charges – the target company will be exposed to a harsh and expensive set of repercussions. These will range from customer desertion and brand damage to significant penalties and operating requirements imposed by their acquiring bank, which will include a future level of monitoring at a level normal only for the very largest of merchants.

PCI DSS is designed to ensure that merchants are effectively protecting cardholder data. It recognises that not all merchants may have the technical understanding to identify for themselves the necessary steps and short-circuits to avoid danger. All merchants, and their service providers, should therefore ensure that they comply with PCI DSS, and that they stay compliant.

Apart from anything else, if every merchant co-operates in the fight against the theft of cardholder data, we might make it easier in the long run for all our payment card customers.

ABOUT THE AUTHORS

Alan Calder is a leading author on IT governance and information security issues. He is Chief Executive of IT Governance Limited, the one-stop-shop for books, tools, training and consultancy on governance, risk management and compliance.

Alan is an international authority on information security management and on ISO27001 (formerly BS7799), the international security standard, about which he wrote with colleague Steve Watkins the definitive compliance guide, *IT Governance: A Manager's Guide to Data Security and BS7799/ISO17799*. This work is based on his experience of leading the world's first successful implementation of BS7799 (with the 4th edition published in May 2008) and is the basis for the UK Open University's postgraduate course on information security.

Other books written by Alan include *The Case for ISO27001* and *ISO27001 – Nine Steps to Success*, as well as several pocket guides in this series.

Alan is a frequent media commentator on information security and IT governance issues, and has contributed articles and expert comment to a wide range of trade, national and online news outlets.

Nicki Carter gained 12 years' experience in the Ministry of Defence and HMG, four years of which were occupied as an Information Security Adviser for government and MOD information systems. Most significantly, Nicki occupied the position of a Qualified Security Assessor (QSA) undertaking Payment Card Industry Data Security Standard (PCI DSS) assessments. The QSA responsibilities included facilitating scoping workshops, gap/risk analysis activities, and undertaking audits with both high-profile public and private sector companies.

Rob Freeman has been responsible for the revision of this guide to reflect the changes and updates contained in the PCI DSS v2.0 standard. Rob has over 15 years' experience working in commercial and technical roles in the electronics, software and information security industry sectors. He has been involved in a number of major projects associated with PCI DSS training and staff awareness programmes.

ACKNOWLEDGEMENTS

The PCI DSS, copies of which are freely available (although subject to licence) from the PCI Security Standards Council (PCI SSC), is, of course, their copyright. This pocket guide is not a substitute for acquiring and reading the standard itself. Every reader of this pocket guide should obtain a copy from:
www.pcisecuritystandards.org/security_standards/documents.php.

This pocket guide contains many references to, and summaries of, material that is freely and more comprehensively available on the PCI SSC website and elsewhere; it is intended to be a handy, comprehensive reference tool that contains in one place all the information that anyone dealing with the PCI DSS and related issues might need. It is also a pocket guide, not a comprehensive manual[1] on implementing PCI DSS.

---

[1] If you are looking for a comprehensive PCI DSS implementation manual, one is available at
www.itgovernance.co.uk/products/1633

CONTENTS

CHAPTER 1: WHAT IS THE PAYMENT CARD INDUSTRY DATA SECURITY STANDARD (PCI DSS)?

The Payment Card Industry Data Security Standard (PCI DSS) was developed by the founding payment brands of the PCI Security Standards Council (PCI SSC, at *www.pcisecuritystandards.org*), including American Express, Discover Financial Services, JCB International, MasterCard Worldwide and Visa.

PCI DSS consists of a standardised, industry-wide set of requirements and processes for security management, policies, procedures, network architecture, software design and critical protective measures.

The PCI DSS must be met by all organisations (merchants and service providers) that transmit, process or store payment card data. The PCI DSS (sometimes referred to as a compliance standard) is not a law. It is a contractual obligation applied and enforced – by means of fines or other restrictions – directly by the payment providers themselves.

The currently applicable version of PCI DSS, since 28 October 2010, is version 2.0; subject to licence, it can be freely downloaded[2]. It is

---

2

www.pcisecuritystandards.org/security_standards/documents.php

published and controlled by the independent PCI Security Standards Council (SSC) on behalf of its five founding members. The SSC also defines qualifications for Qualified Security Assessors (QSAs) and Approved Scanning Vendors (ASVs); and it trains, tests and certifies QSAs and ASVs.

The PCI DSS is a set of 12 requirements that are imposed on merchants and other related parties. These 12 requirements are described later in this pocket guide.

Key definitions[3] and acronyms in the PCI DSS:

Acquirer – Bank, which acquires merchants – i.e. the bank with which you have your e-commerce bank account.

Payment brand – Visa, MasterCard, Amex, Discover, JCB.

Merchant – Sells products to cardholders.

Service provider – A business entity directly involved in the processing, storage, transmission, and switching of cardholder data. This includes companies that provide services to merchants, service providers or members that control or could impact the security of cardholder data.

---

[3] There is a formal English glossary available at *www.pcisecuritystandards.org/documents/pci_glossary_v20.pdf*

1: What is the Payment Card Industry Data Security Standard (PCI DSS)?

Service providers include:

TTPs – Third Party Processors – who process payment card transactions (including payment gateways).

DSEs – Data Storage Entities – who store or transmit payment card data.

QSA – Qualified Security Assessor – someone who is trained and certified to carry out PCI DSS compliance assessments.

ASV – Approved Scanning Vendor – an organisation that is approved as competent to carry out the security scans required by PCI DSS.

PAN – Primary Account Number (the 16 digit payment card number).

CHAPTER 2: WHAT IS THE SCOPE OF THE PCI DSS?

The PCI DSS is applicable if you store, process or transmit cardholder data. The Cardholder Data Environment (CDE) is any network that possesses cardholder data or sensitive authentication data. It does *not* apply to your organisation if Primary Account Numbers (PANs) – the 16-digit credit card numbers – are not stored, processed or transmitted. The PCI DSS applies to any type of media on which card data may be held – this includes hard disk drives, floppy disks, magnetic tape and back-up media, but also embraces printed/handwritten credit and debit card receipts where the full card number is printed. These receipts are often held by merchants as a paper record of the transaction and may be used for voucher recovery purposes or as evidence of the transaction if the acquirer issues a request for information (RFI). The card number must be held in full and therefore the receipts must be stored securely.

Retailers must also secure all other areas where card details may be stored, processed or transmitted. For example, many EPOS systems take a copy of the card details (either swiped separately, or extracted from EFT receipt data) and store them unencrypted within their own databases for reconciliation and reporting purposes.

PCI DSS applies to all system components, including network components, servers, or applications that are included in or connected to the cardholder data environment. It also applies to telephone recording technology used by call centres which accept payment card transactions. Shopping carts and payment processing facilities are examples of applications to which PCI DSS applies (also see the section on the Payment Application Data Security Standard (PA-DSS), later).

While not a specific requirement, PCI DSS strongly recommends that any merchant or service provider reduces the scope of its Cardholder Data Environment (CDE). This reduces the cost and complexity of both the initial assessment and the maintenance of PCI controls. Reducing the scope is typically achieved by isolating (network segmenting) the CDE. Given the complexity of modern IT networks and applications, we would advise that you seek the advice of a qualified PCI DSS consultant prior to completing this activity.

CHAPTER 3: COMPLIANCE AND COMPLIANCE PROGRAMMES

Payment brands enforce the compliance process through contractual means, including higher processing fees, fines and financial penalties.

'What are the consequences to my business if I do not comply with the PCI DSS?'

'The PCI Security Standards Council encourages all businesses that store payment account data to comply with the PCI DSS to help lower their brand and financial risks associated with account payment data compromises. The PCI Security Standards Council does not manage compliance programmes and does not impose any consequences for non-compliance. Individual payment brands, however, may have their own compliance initiatives, including financial or operational consequences to certain businesses that are not compliant.

This all means that each payment provider will take whatever action it thinks it can make stick, commercially, to enforce the PCI DSS. There are no standardised penalties across all the payment brands, and the PCI Council has no plans to create any. Each brand will require separate evidence of compliance and, given that the original dates for compliance have now all passed, is likely to set different dates for different levels and different entities to demonstrate compliance. The acquiring bank is usually the best channel through which to discuss compliance deadlines and penalties, which are all imposed by means of the payment brand/acquiring bank's contract with the merchant.

While the PCI DSS is a common standard, each payment brand has its own compliance programme. Note that there may be regional variations for VISA (e.g. USA and Europe), while MasterCard has a single global standard, and that acquiring banks – not the payment brands – are usually responsible for enforcement. All detailed compliance enquiries should therefore be directed to one's acquiring bank. Detailed below are the websites for the PCI DSS compliance programmes for each of the five founding members of the PCI DSS Council, which will give some guidance on the compliance actions that might be expected in respect of each of the payment brands:

Amex DSOP –

https://www209.americanexpress.com/merchant/si nglevoice/dsw/FrontServlet?request_type=dsw&p g_nm=merchinfo&ln=en&frm=US&intsearchct= curated

Discover Card DISC –

www.discovernetwork.com/fraudsecurity/disc.html

JCB Card PCI DSS –

www.jcb-global.com/english/pci/index.html

MasterCard SDP –

www.mastercard.com/us/sdp/index.html

VISA US CISP –

http://usa.visa.com/merchants/risk_management/cisp_overview.html?it=l2/merchants/risk_management/cisp_merchants.html/Overview

VISA EUROPE AIS –

www.visaeurope.com/aboutvisa/security/ais/main.jsp

VISA ASIA AIS –

www.visa-asia.com/ap/sea/merchants/riskmgmt/ais.shtml

CHAPTER 4: CONSEQUENCES OF A BREACH

The consequences of a data security breach are likely to be proportionate to the seriousness of the breach and the extent to which the merchant is able to demonstrate prior compliance with PCI DSS. For level one merchants, the combinations of fines, litigation and brand damage are significant; for non-level one merchants, the consequences of a breach are potentially as serious and might include:

- There will be a significant cost for a forensic investigation.
- The merchant automatically becomes a level one merchant (i.e. yearly on-site audits).
- There may be a charge by issuer(s) to acquirer(s) for card re-issue, which may be passed on to the merchant.
- The merchant may possibly lose its ability to accept payment cards.

CHAPTER 5: HOW DO YOU COMPLY WITH THE REQUIREMENTS OF THE STANDARD?

All organisations must comply. There are two options for demonstrating compliance: an annual on-site security audit and a quarterly network scan or completion of a Self-Assessment Questionnaire, in some cases together with an annual network scan. Which option applies to any one organisation is determined by transaction volume and whether or not there has previously been a security breach.

Two groups of organisations must demonstrate compliance with PCI DSS: merchants and service providers.

Merchant PCI DSS compliance criteria

Compliance requirements are dependent on a merchant's activity level. There are four levels, based on the annual number of credit/debit card transactions. While payment brands determine the compliance levels for their own brands, acquirers are usually responsible for determining the compliance validation requirement levels of their merchants. The compliance levels are based on the following table and usually refer to the number of transactions of each payment brand in a year. Whether or not transaction volume applies only to e-commerce transactions or to payments processed through all channels is decided separately by each payment brand but, in general, all transactions are included.

Figure 1: Merchant PCI DSS compliance levels

Level one criteria:

Merchants with over six million transactions a year, or merchants whose data has previously been compromised.

Level one validation requirements:

Annual on-site security audit (reviewed by a QSA or internal audit if signed by officer of merchant company and pre-approved by acquirer) and quarterly network security scan.

Level two criteria:

Merchants with between one and six million transactions a year.

Level two validation requirements:

Annual Self-Assessment Questionnaire.

Quarterly scan by an Approved Scanning Vendor (ASV).

Level three criteria:

Merchants with between 20,000 and one million transactions a year.

Level three validation requirements:

Quarterly scan by an Approved Scanning Vendor (ASV).

Annual Self-Assessment Questionnaire.

Level four criteria:

Merchants with less than 20,000 transactions – and the PCI Council are clear that PCI DSS compliance is required even if there is only one payment card transaction per year[4].

Level four validation requirements:

Annual Self-Assessment Questionnaire.

Quarterly scan by an Approved Scanning Vendor (ASV) (may be recommended or required, depending on acquirer compliance criteria).

---

[4] *https://www.pcisecuritystandards.org/documents/pciscc_ten_common_myths.pdf*(Myth 7).

Service provider PCI DSS compliance criteria

A service provider is an organisation that is involved in the processing, storage, transmission and switching of transaction data and/or cardholder information, but is not a merchant or a card brand member. Hosting providers and others providing services to merchants would also fall into this category.

Service provider compliance requirements are defined by the payment brands. Visa and MasterCard categorise service providers according to transaction volume and/or type of service provider. In comparison to the four levels of merchant compliance criteria, there are only two for service providers.

Figure 2: Service provider PCI DSS compliance levels

Level one criteria:

Visa – VisaNet processors, or any service provider that stores, processes and/or transmits over 300,000 Visa transactions annually.

MasterCard – All Third Party Processors (TPPs). All Data Storage Entities (DSEs) that store, transmit, or process greater than 300,000 total combined MasterCard and Maestro transactions annually. All compromised TPPs and DSEs.

<table>
<tr><td>

Level one validation requirements:

Visa and MasterCard – Annual onsite review by a QSA. Quarterly network scan by an ASV.

</td></tr>
<tr><td>

Level two criteria:

Visa – Any service provider that stores, processes and/or transmits less than 300,000 Visa transactions annually.

MasterCard – All DSEs that store, transmit, or process less than combined MasterCard and Maestro transactions annually.

Level two validation requirements:

Visa and MasterCard – Annual Self-Assessment Questionnaire. Quarterly network scan by an ASV.

</td></tr>
</table>

Role of service providers

Many service providers deliver payment services directly to merchants using a variety of online and physical technologies. These services include online payment gateways, traditional document processing facilities and shared hosted server and application providers. PCI DSS asks that shared hosting providers ensure compliance with additional requirements that include protecting each merchant's hosted individual CDE, ensuring availability of audit trails and allowing forensic investigation if required. To achieve compliance with PCI DSS, a merchant must ensure that any service provider that it uses must be PCI DSS compliant.

Service providers demonstrate their compliance to PCI DSS with criteria as outlined in Figure 2. PCI DSS recommends that, in addition to achieving compliance to the requirements of the standard, service providers should also prove to merchants that they are compliant by the provision of supporting evidence.

Online payment gateways

For merchants who sell their products or services online on a website, we strongly recommend the use of a third party payment gateway service which is fully PCI compliant. These services are available from PayPal, SagePay, WorldPay, HSBC Secure ePayments and Barclays ePDQ. For the smaller e-commerce business, outsourcing to a payment gateway service provides a very cost effective way of ensuring PCI compliance. Please note that such a merchant (likely to be Level 3 or 4) will be required to complete the relevant Self Assessment Questionnaire (SAQ)and a submit the results of a quarterly scan by an Approved Scanning Vendor. The SAQ document required will either be SAQ C or the newer SAQ C-VT which applies to merchants that use Web-based virtual terminals to manually enter payment card information. See Chapter 9, Figure 3 for further information.

CHAPTER 6: MAINTAINING COMPLIANCE

Once an organisation has achieved compliance with the PCI DSS, it must maintain its level of compliance. This, of course, means making oneself aware of any changes to the PCI DSS itself (the latest version was released in October 2010), as well as maintaining the PCI DSS security environment.

The PCI Council makes the point this way: Technically, it is true that, if you've completed a Self-Assessment Questionnaire (SAQ), you're compliant – 'for that particular moment in time when the Self-Assessment Questionnaire and associated vulnerability scan (if applicable) is completed. After that moment, only a post-breach forensic analysis can prove PCI compliance. But a bad system change can make you non-compliant in an instant. True security of payment card data requires non-stop assessment and remediation to ensure that the likelihood of a breach is kept as low as possible.'[5]

---

[5] *https://www.pcisecuritystandards.org/documents/p ciscc_ten_common_myths.pdf*(Myth 8).

CHAPTER 7: PCI DSS – THE STANDARD

The PCI DSS has 12 requirements, organised into six sections. Please note that this pocket guide is no substitute for obtaining your own copy of the standard, which is freely downloadable from *www.pcisecuritystandards.org/security_standards/documents.php*.

PCI DSS version 1.0 was originally published in January 2005, with subsequent updates to version 1.1 in September 2006 and version 1.2 in October 2008. The current version is PCI DSS v2.0 which was released on 28 October 2010.

With the release of PCI DSS v2.0, the PCI Security Standards Council has introduced a new three-year lifecycle for standards development. This ensures a gradual and phased introduction of new version, and helps to prevent organisations from becoming non-compliant when a new standard is published.

The 12 PCI DSS requirements, and the six principles in which those requirements are grouped, are as follows:

Build and maintain a secure network

Requirement 1: Install and maintain a firewall configuration to protect cardholder data.

Requirement 2: Do not use vendor-supplied defaults for system passwords and other security parameters.

Protect cardholder data

Requirement 3: Protect stored cardholder data.

Requirement 4: Encrypt transmission of cardholder data across open, public networks.

Maintain a vulnerability management programme

Requirement 5: Use and regularly update anti-virus software or programs.

Requirement 6: Develop and maintain secure systems and applications.

Implement strong access control measures

Requirement 7: Restrict access to cardholder data by business need-to-know.

Requirement 8: Assign a unique ID to each person with computer access.

Requirement 9: Restrict physical access to cardholder data.

Regularly monitor and test networks

Requirement 10: Track and monitor all access to network resources and cardholder data.

Requirement 11: Regularly test security systems and processes.

Maintain an information security policy

Requirement 12: Maintain a policy that addresses information security for employees and contractors.

CHAPTER 8: ASPECTS OF PCI DSS COMPLIANCE

Requirement 1 (Install and maintain a firewall configuration to protect cardholder data)

- Create and maintain firewall configuration standards.
- Consider placement of DMZ and firewalls.
- Restrict inbound/outbound traffic.
- Develop network diagrams.

Requirement 2 (Do not use vendor-supplied defaults for system passwords and other security parameters)

- Change all vendor default passwords.
- Develop and implement configuration standards for all system components.
- Remove unnecessary functionality.

Requirement 3 (Protect stored cardholder data)

- Data retention and disposal policy.
- Do not store sensitive authentication data post authorisation, including security code (CVV2 etc.), magnetic stripe (track 1/track 2) or the Personal Identification number (PIN) or encrypted PIN block.
- Mask the PAN when displayed.
- Render the PAN unreadable anywhere it is stored.
- Document key management processes and procedures for keys used for the encryption of cardholder data.

Requirement 4 (Encrypt transmission of cardholder data across open, public networks)

- Applies to transmission of cardholder data over all open, public networks (the Internet is an open, public network).
- Wireless networks are particularly insecure and need specific attention.

Requirement 5 (Use and regularly update anti-virus software or programs)

- Anti-malware software must deal with everything, including spyware and so on.
- Ensure this software is current, actively running, and capable of generating logs.

Requirement 6 (Develop and maintain secure systems and applications)

- Install vendor-supplied security patches, preferably on an automated basis.
- Change control procedures are required, as are software development processes (if you develop software).
- Develop Web applications based on secure coding guidelines (e.g. OWASP).
- Protect web applications by:
  - Having the code reviewed by a specialist organisation.
  - An application-layer firewall.

Requirement 7 (Restrict access to cardholder data by business need-to-know)

- Apply least privileges required for actual job responsibilities.

- Access rights should be based on user's need-to-know and set to 'deny all', unless specifically allowed.

Requirement 8 (Assign a unique ID to each person with computer access)

- Unique IDs and authentication methods (passwords/token devices/biometrics) should be used for everyone.
- Prohibit group/shared/generic accounts.
- Two-factor authentication should be standard for remote access.
- Create (and use) an authorisation form for all users.

Requirement 9 (Restrict physical access to cardholder data)

- The payment card environment should have physical security controls.
- There should be procedures for the identification and management of staff/visitors.
- Media protection, control and destruction procedures are required.

Requirement 10 (Track and monitor all access to network resources and cardholder data)

- Audit trails should be created that will enable you to reconstruct and record events.
- Synchronise system clocks, including laptops, mobiles, etc.

Requirement 11 (Regularly test security systems and processes)

- All devices should be tested (e.g. wireless analyser).
- Internal and external network vulnerability scans are required (at least quarterly).
- Penetration testing (network and application layer) is required.
- Network and host-based IDS or IPS.
- File integrity monitoring.

Requirement 12 (Maintain a policy that addresses information security for employees and contractors)

- Information security policy.
- Education and training of employees and contractors is essential.
- Screen potential employees and contractors.
- Ensure that PCI DSS requirements are spelt out in contracts with service providers.

When an organisation is unable to meet the strict requirements of PCI DSS, due to legitimate or documented business constraints, it is permissible to submit a number of alternative measures. These measures are known as compensating controls and must fully mitigate the risks associated with the requirements and meet the criteria as defined in Appendix B: Compensating Controls of the PCI DSS standard.

CHAPTER 9: THE PCI SELF-ASSESSMENT QUESTIONNAIRE (SAQ)

The PCI Data Security Standard Self-Assessment Questionnaire is a validation tool developed by the PCI Council to assist merchants and service providers in self-evaluating their compliance with the Payment Card Industry Data Security Standard (PCI DSS).

All merchants and their service providers are required to comply with the PCI Data Security Standard in its entirety and, if they are eligible for self-assessment, to attest that they comply by using the standard Attestation of Compliance document. In October 2010, the PCI Security Standards Council introduced a new Self-Assessment Questionnaire (and the Attestation of Compliance) that is in line with version 2.0 of the PCI DSS.

There are now five validation categories for this questionnaire (*see Figure 3 following*), each of which can be downloaded from: *www.pcisecuritystandards.org/documents/pci_dss _saq_instr_guide_v2.0.pdf.*

Figure 3: Self-Assessment Questionnaire validation categories

SAQ validation type	Description
A	Card-not-present (e-commerce or mail/telephone order) merchants, for whom all cardholder data functions are outsourced. This would never apply to face-to-face merchants.
B	Imprint-only merchants with no electronic cardholder data storage, or standalone, dial-out terminal merchants with no electronic cardholder data storage.
C-VT	Merchants using web-based virtual terminals; no electronic cardholder data storage.
C	Merchants with payment application systems connected to the Internet, but no electronic cardholder data storage.
D	All other merchants not included in SAQ types above, and all service providers defined by a payment brand as eligible to complete an SAQ.

CHAPTER 10: PROCEDURES AND QUALIFICATIONS

The PCI Council mandates the procedures that must be followed in conducting audits and in carrying out scanning procedures. It also lays down specific requirements for qualification as a QSA or an ASV.

PCI DSS Validation Requirements for Qualified Security Assessors (QSAs) v 1.2.

(www.pcisecuritystandards.org/documents/qsa_va lidation_requirements.pdf)

To be recognised as a QSA by the PCI SSC, QSAs must meet or exceed the requirements described in the above document and must also execute the QSA Agreement with the PCI Council below. Clients can provide feedback on the effectiveness of the QSA.

PCI Qualified Security Assessor (QSA) Agreement

(www.pcisecuritystandards.org/documents/qsa_va lidation_requirements.pdf)

Sample QSA Feedback Form

(www.pcisecuritystandards.org/documents/qsa_fee dback_form_-_client.pdf)

PCI DSS Qualified Security Assessors

*(www.pcisecuritystandards.org/approved_compan
ies_providers/qualified_security_assessors.php)*

This list, which is updated on a regular basis, contains contact details for all Qualified Security Assessors, together with information about the markets they serve.

PCI DSS Validation Requirements for Approved Scanning Vendors (ASVs) v 1.2

*(www.pcisecuritystandards.org/documents/asv_val
idation_requirements.pdf)*

Recognition as an ASV by the PCI Council requires the ASV, its employees, and its scanning solution to meet or exceed the requirements described above and to execute the 'PCI ASV Compliance Test Agreement' set out below with the PCI Council. The companies that qualify are then identified on PCI SSC's ASV list on their website.

PCI ASV Compliance Test Agreement Sample ASV Feedback Form

*(www.pcisecuritystandards.org/documents/asv_fee
dback_form_-_client.pdf)*

PCI DSS Approved Scanning Vendors

*(www.pcisecuritystandards.org/approved_compan
ies_providers/approved_scanning_vendors.php)*

This list, which is updated on a regular basis, contains contact details for all approved ASVs.

Any ASV that carries out a scan must be on the list at the point that the scan is carried out.

ASV Program Guide v1.2

(https://www.pcisecuritystandards.org/documents/ asv_program_guide_v1.0.pdf)

This document provides guidance and requirements applicable to ASVs in the framework of the PCI DSS and associated payment brand data protection programmes. Security scanning companies interested in providing scan services as part of the PCI programme must comply with the requirements set out in this document, and must successfully complete the PCI Security Scanning Vendor Testing and Approval Process.

CHAPTER 11: PCI DSS AND ISO/IEC 27001

ISO/IEC 27001 is the international information security management standard that more and more organisations are using to ensure that their information security management meets the data protection and compliance requirements of a wide variety of legislation, including the EU Data Protection Acts and Privacy Directives, HIPAA, GLBA and others.

While the PCI standard was not written to map specifically to ISO27001 or to any other existing framework, it sits clearly within the ISO27001 framework, and organisations that have implemented an ISO27001 ISMS should be able, with minor additional work, to also demonstrate their conformance with the PCI standard. The individual controls set out in detail inside the PCI DSS can be mapped[6] to the controls and clauses of ISO27001 (primarily to Annex A, the list of information security controls).

It certainly makes sense for any organisation that is pursuing either ISO27001 or PCI DSS, and has both payment card data and other confidential data (whether personally identifiable information – sometimes known as 'PID') or other commercial

---

[6] A document that maps the individual clauses of the PCI DSS v2.0 to the individual clauses of ISO/IEC 27001 Annex A is available to IT Governance subscribers within the online KnowledgeBank (subscriptions available from _www.itgovernance.co.uk/products/223_).

information to protect, to tackle the requirements of PCI DSS from within the ISO27001 framework.

34

CHAPTER 12: PAYMENT APPLICATION DATA SECURITY STANDARD (PA-DSS)

PA-DSS is the PCI Council managed programme that focuses on payment applications, such as shopping carts, payment gateways, and so on. This programme was previously run by Visa Inc. and was known as Payment Application Best Practices (PABP). Increasingly, criminals are targeting vulnerabilities in payment applications to steal payment card data, and some software may be storing sensitive card data on a user's system unknowingly. PA-DSS is therefore meant to help software vendors and others develop secure payment applications that do not store prohibited data, such as full magnetic stripes, CVV2 or PIN data, and to ensure their payment applications support compliance with the PCI DSS.

Payment applications that are sold, distributed or licensed to third parties are subject to the PA-DSS requirements. In-house payment applications that are developed by merchants or service providers and which are not sold to a third party are not subject to the PA-DSS requirements, but must still comply with PCI DSS.

PA-DSS has its own security audit procedures[7] and its own detailed programme guide[8] that help

---

[7] *www.pcisecuritystandards.org/documents/pa-dss_v2.pdf*

[8] *www.pcisecuritystandards.org/documents/pci_pa_dss_program_guide.pdf*

organisations determine exactly how these compliance requirements affect them. The PCI Security Standards Council also publishes and maintains a list of Validated Payment Applications[9] that have been assessed as having met the requirements of the standard. As this list is continually being updated, we recommend that merchants contact the respective software vendors to confirm that their applications are fully compliant with PA-DSS.

As mentioned in Chapter 5, we strongly recommend the use of a third party payment gateway service which is fully PCI compliant particularly for the requirements of a small e-commerce business. While such a service provider is not obliged to use an in-house software application which is compliant to PA-DSS, we would advise that merchants use the larger suppliers who are fully compliant with PA-DSS and PCI DSS.

---

[9] *www.pcisecuritystandards.org/approved_compani es_providers/vpa_agreement.php*

CHAPTER 13: PIN TRANSACTION SECURITY (PTS))

The PCI Council also has compliance requirements for pin entry (pin pad and point-of-sale) devices that are used in conjunction with payment cards in environments attended by a cashier, merchant or sales clerk. There is a testing and approval guide and a list of approved devices, together with detailed vendor guidance on how to gain approval. All this information is available at *www.pcisecuritystandards.org/security_standards/documents.php?association=PTS*.

The PIN Transaction Security programme includes unattended payment terminals (UPTs) and hardware security modules (HSMs), so that these devices can be rigorously tested to ensure they secure cardholder data in a payment process. UPTs are unattended payment devices that include self-service ticketing machines, kiosks, automated fuel pumps and vending machines. HSMs are secure cryptographic devices that can be used for PIN translation, card personalisation, electronic commerce or data protection and do not include any type of cardholder interface. The PCI Council maintains a list of approved UPTs and HSMs.

ITG RESOURCES

IT Governance Ltd. sources, creates and delivers products and services to meet the real-world, evolving IT governance needs of today's organisations, directors, managers and practitioners.

The ITG website (*www.itgovernance.co.uk*) is the international one-stop-shop for corporate and IT governance information, advice, guidance, books, tools, training and consultancy.

http://www.itgovernance.co.uk/pci_dss.aspx is the information page on our website for our PCI DSS resources.

Other Websites

Books and tools published by IT Governance Publishing (ITGP) are available from all business booksellers and are also immediately available from the following websites:

www.itgovernance.co.uk/catalog/355 provides information and online purchasing facilities for every currently available book published by ITGP.

www.itgovernanceusa.com is a US$-based website that delivers the full range of IT Governance products to North America, and ships from within the continental US.

www.itgovernanceasia.com provides a selected range of ITGP products specifically for customers in South Asia.

www.27001.com is the IT Governance Ltd. website that deals specifically with information security management, and ships from within the continental US.

Pocket Guides

For full details of the entire range of IT Governance pocket guides, simply follow the links at *www.itgovernance.co.uk/catalog/279*. You can also find more books on PCI DSS compliance, including a detailed implementation manual, at *www.itgovernance.co.uk/products/1633*.

Toolkits

ITG's unique range of toolkits includes the PCI DSS Toolkit, which contains all the tools and guidance that you will need in order to meet the requirements of the PCI DSS Self-Assessment Questionnaire. Full details can be found at *www.itgovernance.co.uk/products/1337*.

For a free paper on how to use the proprietary Calder-Moir IT Governance Framework to integrate all aspects of your information security and IT governance activities, and for a free trial version of the IT Governance Framework Toolkit, see *www.itgovernance.co.uk/products/519.*

PCI ASV Scanning Service

The PCI HackerGuardian Scanning Service supplied by IT Governance satisfies the required quarterly Vulnerability Scanning certification and report requirements of the PCI DSS. This service is delivered by Comodo, which is a PCI Approved Scanning Vendor. For further information, please see *www.itgovernance.co.uk/pci-scanning.aspx.*

Best Practice Reports

ITG's range of Best Practice Reports is now at *www.itgovernance.co.uk/best-practice-reports.aspx*. These offer you essential, pertinent, expertly researched information on an increasing number of key issues including Web 2.0 and Green IT.

Training and Consultancy

IT Governance also offers training and consultancy services across the entire spectrum of disciplines in the information governance arena, including, in particular, support around PCI DSS compliance. Details of training courses – including our respected one-day PCI foundation training course – can be accessed at *www.itgovernance.co.uk/products/1858* and a description of our PCI DSS consultancy support services can be found at *www.itgovernance.co.uk/pci-consultancy.aspx.* Why not contact us to see how we could help you and your organisation?

Newsletter

IT governance is one of the hottest topics in business today, not least because it is also the fastest moving, so what better way to keep up than by subscribing to ITG's free monthly newsletter *Sentinel*? It provides monthly updates and resources across the whole spectrum of IT governance subject matter, including risk management, information security, ITIL and IT service management, project governance, compliance and so much more. Subscribe for your free copy at: *www.itgovernance.co.uk/newsletter.aspx*.